WHO IS TRIXIE THE TRASHER? AND OTHER QUESTIONS

Also by Jane Miller

Who Is Trixie the Trasher?
and Other Questions

Poems by
JANE MILLER

 Copper Canyon Press
Port Townsend, Washington

Cover art: Cecily Brown, *Service de Luxe*, 1999

Copper Canyon Press is in residence at Fort Worden State Park in Port Townsend,
Washington, under the auspices of Centrum. Centrum is a gathering place for artists and
creative thinkers from around the world, students of all ages and backgrounds, and
audiences seeking extraordinary cultural enrichment.

LIBRARY OF CONGRESS CATALOGING-IN-PUBLICATION DATA

Names: Miller, Jane, 1949– author
Title: Who is Trixie the Trasher? and other questions : poems / by Jane Miller.
Description: Port Townsend, Washington : Copper Canyon Press, 2018.
Identifiers: LCCN 2018016184 | ISBN 9781556595400 (pbk. : alk. paper)
Classification: LCC PS3563.I4116 A6 2018 | DDC 811/.54—dc23
LC record available at https://lccn.loc.gov/2018016184

9 8 7 6 5 4 3 2 FIRST PRINTING

Copper Canyon Press
Post Office Box 271
Port Townsend, Washington 98368

www.coppercanyonpress.org

for Valyntina

Acknowledgments

Grateful acknowledgment to editors of the following journals in which some of these poems first appeared: *Bat City Review; Fence; Lana Turner: A Journal of Poetry and Opinion; The New Yorker; Poetry; The Volta.*

I mention Walgreens in "Who Is Trixie the Trasher?" to honor (however peripherally) Ruth Walgreen Stephan, writer, editor, philanthropist, who founded the University of Arizona Poetry Center.

"Or Else?" was written in response to C.D. Wright's "The Obscure Lives of Poets." My poem starts where hers broke off:

> we get ourselves up, off our much abused sofas,
> Hermanos, Hermanas, to the old intolerable sound of hollow spoons in hollow bowls,
> to insure that our love has not left the world or else

"Whether the Goat Is a Metaphor," based on the Russian folktale "Sister Alyonushka and Brother Ivanushka" (in *Vasilisa the Beautiful: Russian Fairy Tales,* edited by Irina Zheleznova), was written to accompany one of Yuliya Lanina's marvelous mechanical sculptures. She makes fictive universes inhabited by half-human, half-animal demigods living in music boxes, with melodies by the composer Yevgeniy Sharlat. Exhibited 2016, at CAMIBAart Gallery, Austin, Texas.

Italicized lines in "What Is Virtue?" are from "Timely Warning: aggravated assault with a knife," University of Texas Police Department notification provided in accordance with the Jeanne Clery Disclosure of Campus Security Policy and Campus Crime Statistics Act, 20 U.S.C., §1092(f), and from the National Weather Service, May 23, 2016.

"Who Is Trixie the Trasher?" is for Lisa Olstein.

"Whether to Buy Whiskey, Guns, and Ammo" is for Dean Young.

"White Poppies and Purple Thistles" is for Susan Briante, Farid Matuk, Megan Campbell, and Ander Monson.

Thank you for your devotion, Michael Wiegers. Elaina Ellis, thank you for your precise readings of this work in manuscript.

Thank you for years of sustaining love: Mona Vold, Jorie Graham, Peter Sacks, Lisa Schlesinger, Jacqi Tully, Beth Aboulafia, Deb Gregerman, Caryn Miller, Olga Broumas, Jane Mead, Caroline Duncan, Pedro Moreno, Lisa and Victoria Garza, Sandra and Christopher Osborne, and Melanie and Peter Maier.

In memoriam, Sam Hamill, to whom I owe a thousand thanks.

CONTENTS

WHO IS TRIXIE THE TRASHER? AND OTHER QUESTIONS

OUTSHINES ITS CANOPY OF INTENT

We were up late and everyone had been drinking, and someone said, Hey, is that God's
head on the boil?
We didn't know where to look or what to think, it was obviously some sort of perverse
joke, or not, right?
And the conversation went on for days, thirsty, sober, asleep, awake, what did it matter?
Some of us felt the real time was *for* something, but what?
And the questions kept coming, once they started, my favorite one being two strung
together, What makes art "modern" and what does "urgent" mean now?
Where was the greater good? That was another worry bandied about,
followed by Where was the common tent? which gave a feeling of empathy for a minute
and then grief because, well, where was it?
Will you arm, hoard seeds, go hungry? Those terrified me because, after all, who will
repair things when the end is pale or dark?
Where will you hide out

when capital runs out, when water? Which will be greater, the heat or the cold?
Wait, did God's boiling head just say something? Cry out *Go to hell* from a giant lobster
pot? Tantalizing us with where to go next?
Are phosphorescent lamps to mark escape paths?
Not that it's not a great party, but whose place is this? Igniting
quail in banana leaves, sons bandaged, who invited us?
Why are the emerald bleeding and the ivory weeping? (Lower the freaking music.)
Does anyone have the time?

TIME OUT

When did the day turn unimaginable?

It was time to admit the heir to the throne into the ladies' room

When did you refute the pop-up president?

After a mellow ride through the countryside on a bicycle

When did you finish? Did you finish?

Yes, as soon as the river ran backwards through the marketplace

When could you not respond?

About the same time I realized the Judeo-Christian tradition was as shrill as a buzz saw

Did you abandon your goal?

I slept in the middle of the bed under a window until enough was enough

When was morality born of intimidation?

An hour after our leader loaded the cats onto the boats

Where was your foothold?

Right here in this picture of myself holding a kettle over an open flame

If it was too hot to walk, why did you speed up?

Because when something is dead in nature, the dead are happiest there

When is your answer unimaginative?

If I get along really well with you but it no longer matters

Why must desire be sacrificed for security? Is it sacrificed?

Yes, because a denuded forest cannot be considered rustic

When did you lose your appetite?

After wondering what makes a great book

Where were you when you threw it for a loop?

On a yellow couch in a downpour

When did you lose interest?

I was giving a lecture on swamps

When was the jury trial?

After the defendant folded whatever happened into smaller pieces

What hope remains?

At the end of the play the audience bowed until dawn

When did you run out of food?

I had barely taken the long trail around three limestone outcroppings

At what point did it stop raining?

Right after the cliff appeared to move a couple of miles west

When did you get thin?

As soon as I heard the commandments recited in a grand manner

Where were you when it passed?

We had all recently been to Torchy's Tacos

To whom went the spoils?

Those standing nearest the coconut trees had the advantage

Why did you lose your direction?

My relatives died on the same day in different years

When did the banks close down?

No sooner than the brightest star switched constellations

When did the mufflings and insinuations begin?

I realized I'd never be young again so I bought a ticket

What was your biggest problem?

Robots who don't inspire but humiliate

Your biggest terror?

That I have forgotten

POM POM ROOM

Do we really have to go into these feelings?

It's all about an object of desire

A tutu pierced by a thought

All about that time

I could have loved you forever

It's about the prospect of death

Amphorae, statues, mirrors, coins, honey, and amber

All about geography

Suddenly a hard rain pounds a balmy afternoon

About behaving as if you can predict the future

Allergens of oak and grass

All about someone satisfying and frustrating us

Someone's claim to our sovereignty

All about that martini

Never quite as obedient as we seem to be

About that sexuality confusion

Our most sadomasochistic way of seeing ourselves

It's about a too-simple vocabulary

The loquat girl emerges from her stand

All about mutually informing each other

And later as a woman in an evening gown

About opposing feelings

Having left dishes, pots, and pans in a sink

It's about dropping this relentless critique

Live oaks drip along the road

All about a little waterfall before a performance on a piano

How about that soft light between buildings

When she reappears in twelve poses

I have taken too much of my brother's advice

All about the violence of our preferences

Slave laborers paddle upstream

It's all about shredding that song

Whoever knifes, flays, rapes, and gelds

It's about something dead in the park in the dark

They didn't hear you because they can't hear at all

About loving our neighbors

It's pretending you know people

Truth and beauty still hold sway

It's all about unraveling our history

Are we not required to judge what is wrong with civilization?

SIXTY-SIX WINDOWS

Woman with her hair held in a rough knot by a red twist, mopping, age 29
Woman with her hair held in a rough knot by a red twist, mopping, age 56

Woman half-draped in a towel in a steamy bathroom, age 80
Woman half-draped in a towel in a steamy bathroom, age 25

Age 23, pregnant woman holding her six-year-old's hand
Age 48, pregnant woman holding her six-year-old's hand

White female in police blotter, cropped hair, age 24, scratches on face
Black female in police blotter, cropped hair, age 24, scratches on face

Young woman licking strawberry ice cream at the shoreline
Old woman licking strawberry ice cream at the shoreline

Woman in a burka at an embassy party, in her thirties, in the arms of a woman in her
thirties in military uniform

Age 19, 10 p.m., woman in jeans and a loose blouse studying algorithms in a diner
Age 58, 10 a.m., woman in jeans and a loose blouse studying algorithms in a diner

Applying mascara in bra and underpants in a brightly lit apartment before dressing
for dinner, age 31
Applying mascara in bra and underpants in a brightly lit apartment before dressing
for dinner, age 67

Girl, 16, swimming in a dotted bikini with her bald father
Woman, 19, racing in a blue Speedo missing her dead father

Woman in a gray parka on a bus, age 18, wearing headphones and daydreaming next to
a woman in a gray parka, age 48, wearing headphones and daydreaming

Begging, age 21
Begging, age 81

Woman bicycling with a dog in a basket, 60
Girl bicycling with a dog in a basket, 10

Woman, 79, frantic in a stalled subway car, seated knee-to-knee and gripping hands with a frantic twenty-year-old

Docent, age 50–60?, and two children staring up at a J.M.W. Turner painting
Cotton tenant, age 35–45?, and two children staring out of a Walker Evans photograph

Woman in a cinched coat, age 24, jerking a white guy behind the old bakery
Woman in a cinched coat, age 44, jerking a white guy behind the old bakery

Man with downy facial hair in a sharp suit, age 40
Woman with downy facial hair in a sharp suit, age 40

Girl on crutches, 15
Woman on crutches, 85

Long-haired blond, gender?, in a caftan, age 20–30?, hitchhiking on a freeway
with upright instrument in brown canvas bag (bass? cello?)
Legal guardian, gender?, age 60–70?, in ironed slacks and V-neck sweater, changing
diapers on twins at a convenience store along a freeway

Woman in a green nylon do-rag cleaning toilets in an empty baseball stadium, 22
Woman, veiled, in bare feet, 22

Woman and sunglasses and margarita, 22
Woman and sunglasses and margarita, 32
Woman and sunglasses and margarita, 42
Woman and sunglasses and margarita, 52
Woman and sunglasses and margarita, 62
Woman and sunglasses and margarita, 72

Woman, 44, and man, 27, in an argument at a casino
Transgender mother, 84, with her son, 64, in an argument at a casino
Woman, 40, and woman, 64, in an argument at a casino
Woman with her twin, 29, in an argument at a casino
Woman, 28, and transgender bellhop, 29, in an argument at a casino
Man, 21, and man, 58, in an argument at a casino

Cook in a leather jacket, silk dress, and nose ring at a butcher shop, Paris, age 28
Assistant professor in a leather jacket at a poetry reading, New York, age 28
Trust fund "baby" in a leather jacket at a Cineplex, Tokyo, age 38
Bouncer in a leather jacket in a honky-tonk, Austin, age 38

Undocumented immigrant in a leather jacket, Los Angeles International Airport, age 48
Friend in a leather jacket in a hospital emergency room, middle of nowhere, age 48
Widow in a leather jacket at a railway station, Amsterdam, age 58
Ex-convict in a leather jacket in a snowstorm, Taos, age 58

Black nude on white bedding in a high-rise apartment, age 36, reading
White nude on white bedding in a mid-century modern, age 66, writing

WHO IS TRIXIE THE TRASHER?

Is she a faceless woman using a bidet and chamber pot

bending her backside to you,

legs splayed, maybe masturbating,

naked but for stockings and heels?

Somebody who is all over art history

and also in dire need of money?

Wait a wicked second.

Death, dear reader, is the correct answer,

a metaphor that darkens and makes more common

the young lady in the bathroom

who needs time

to freshen up and dab on a bit of face cream

and cover her stretch marks and bites.

She'd rather go listen to the radio

in bed alone, sing off-key, and sip whiskey slowly.

Trixie, dressed for business as a rare disease,

attack of the heart, nerve-blowing stroke, etc.,

doesn't require your imagination to fuss over her,

or a car and driver,

or some drunk fuck on the street with a money clip

who doesn't know what he's getting into, and can't wait.

As a writer,

by definition having direct access to you here,

however briefly, I grant you every little thing

is passing faster than he can find his dick in his dark suit.

I'm talking about the operator who has been eyeing the poor soul;

she's on the street because frankly it's time for another Joe to blow,

and while he's diddling with his ignorant self I'm doodling that

he's about to die and doesn't realize, because today,

Death is walking the street in tight jeans. Lousy with feminism,

I'm investing her with adamantine fury

that she turns big-time on you

because you're a manifestation, too,

of something before willpower or after

that only the idea of mortality,

and maybe the work of art, can affect.

I've chosen the figure of a denizen

who'd as soon read the news as hunker down

with anything hotter than a coffee.

Eventually, I'd favor nothing

more than to get the girl off the avenue.

Should I put her in a factory,

or at the head of a company

in something Chanel? Unless you see yourself,

you need to stop staring

from your plush booth at Trixie,

who just spilled her espresso

on her inner thigh and cried out,

Holy shit. Why debase/erase you?

I'm assuming everybody has it in her

or him to dehumanize, so I

mash this up and invite a call girl,

a synecdoche, in fact, who helps me with my hoax

poem to fell you like a wall bed.

The power I can give her is her

dignity, by her gaze and upright gait

distanced from craving, which leads to suffering,

which leads to craving, and you paying

with the loss of your best self. For my money,

she'll be sensible, compassionate, and you

won't see her coming to deliver your final blow.

I hate to see you suffer. So, hastily,

right when people all over this town

have their top down, it's a Saturday

(could be you're idly reading poetry), holy

crap, you're pinned by Trixie to a stretcher

that has never, nor will ever,

be thought of as sexy, and whose ancient

calling to haul you away is everywhere

about as perverse as all the places

you've taken this faceless make-up.

I sew your handler into tight pants and hope in a moment

of enlightenment that you also see her

limping and holding her jaw in one hand—

she hasn't the time or money

to get to a dentist for a root canal

or Walgreens for gel pads for her feet.

Everything changes the moment we take pity.

Her tooth is killing her, giving her her

humanity, a provisional victory, and goddamnit, it hurts.

Would you ever catch her at home, washing

her panties before dawn, her dishes,

leveling with you in this sexist world

of male gaze and female fuckability, everyone looking

for a little empathy in the end?

What bit can be learned about a culture

that objectifies death and sex

equally, in an alley or a painting, while a human being—

empowered, devoured, tired, and crying—

too hungry not to hurry after work, drops

her hamburger and fries on the sidewalk?

I'm ashamed. Art may be by nature

manipulative, exploitative, and fallacious

—not ever necessary before

food, water, shelter, and a friend—

but our most distinguished self is not simply anyone

on the cheap who stereotypes, rather more likely

a woman or a man who loves life like nobody's business.

You're being made to think on some level

scaffolding collapsing

that art is a dirty trick, some creep

who crashed and trashed your place,

or in this case your person in this poem.

In my farce, my amiable, unfortunate gaffe,

a deconstructed model delivers the all-powerful consummation

that catches you off guard, bang! with a hammer to the head,

a cartoon image, to be sure, perhaps not a gratuity

that you can afford, but in your wildest imagination

if art means anything, you realize what is represented there

doesn't exist. If there's a murder in a poem, no one calls

the civil guard, which means forms are free to lead

like lampposts down a city block through perversity and degradation

to our higher selves. We get there circuitously. For another thing,

Trixie's cracked a tooth, bringing the goods to you,

so death and beauty are going to need

to be redressed. Your own hot, hot

grad student in a tight knit, in a dirty corner of your mind,

lies beside you in the afterlife of this work, appealing

to your common sense, a Trixie the Trasher

who queer and straight in some measure

desire and postcoital admire

for having the balls to make hard

cold cash quickly. I could have made Death a god,

a razor, a jailer, not the one you are preternaturally

drawn to, with the aches in her foot, mouth, shoulder, her

lips all glowy, skin snowy, hair piled to one side, etc.

Pay no mind. The metaphor loses capacity

after I've had my way with you—art is cruel,

but life is more so. As I lay you outside of time on a cold marble slab

as a sculpture of a human seeing and being seen,

I tire of the game and lend a tired young lady the money

to earn a judgeship and suffer mostly desperate men.

As perverse as you, I'm Trixie's brute but also her witness

and subject. Hell, I can only write

from my wasted heart that no one gets

to possess Trixie. Fantasy is disastrous,

some young soul's harrowing

experience, who dresses her body

in a little black nothing, after a fashion.

She's one lonely bitch, you, scared shitless

in your last minute, blurt. If I were, no harm intended,

a male writer, could I have you

say that? The debasement we fear the most?—Hey,

death has no personal interest in you, a thing of beauty

like a clay pot or a glass bowl. She bows

and puts a liquored cigarette out in your mouth.

Art is righteous loneliness.

WHETHER TO BUY WHISKEY, GUNS, AND AMMO

A couple of old friends, fishing—one's drinking in the boat
with their small catch when the other, having fallen in the sea,
has to be pulled, but also climbs, back in. So easy
to lose someone, and ourselves. They're out there
in some mood, cold, tired, but also preoccupied
with tomorrow, yesterday, and tonight. They're still close,
and they're thinking—I know them—
that after they settle the day's work, they'll pan fry
two golden gray mullets in olive oil, lemon juice, and parsley.
If you prefer, they can cook right on the beach.
It's a matter of great urgency, sad and sexy,
gentle and angry, an appeal against mortality.
Is it any more compelling if an intruder
holds a gun to your head, then changes
his mind? One far out to sea has a view
of the end of things bursting with life.

SWAN HAIR

Was there a murder nearby, talked about all year,

less and less by you

as you quickly drove past others stopped to gawk?

Were you in love at the time?

Was your mother still alive?

Are you dressed now, therefore in public?

Are you walking home alone?

Is it humid? Does it occur to you

that while grasses blow without anyone

observing wind, relationships befall you?

Do you want to be aroused by words,

or does that bore you, like porn?

Are you yourself hungry?

Is there a sense that you're on a floating bed?

Do you think of yourself in an apartment by the sea, winter,

a few neighbors and foghorns, early evening and the mood already gloomy?

Can you recall if anyone helped you?

Do you compare yourself to a passerby

in a loose white blouse and jeans?

Do others shut down nearer your power?

If I think of you, will I draw another breath?

Was there a melon in high season

or a wall when it snowed?

Didn't the tray weigh nothing on your body

when your dearest woke you with a plate of toasts and ginger,

lingering in the room while you dressed in tights, a slip,

and a mustache to be funny?

Did you laugh? Do you forget?

When you made love and smelled of sweat and mint,

did you wake too early? Did it matter?

Did you anticipate your birthday

and the hundreds of people?

Were those slippers, tap shoes, heels, and sneakers

rarely worn because you lay around

in a cloud? Did people want you?

Were you scandalous?

Were you available?

Had you money? Were you thrilled?

Did you cleave? How?

Were you valiant? furtive? masculine?

Were the dishes done? Were you immaculate?

Did you suffer?

Do I know,

if you cried, was it a moment, an hour, or much longer?

Did you never? Do I believe you?

Did you imagine your everyday life

as a frog or victim or swimmer or liar

or a pair of binoculars or a winning ticket?

Is feeling surreal like swan hair?

Was that your city? Were you tired?

Was there shock? Pleasure?

Was there water nearby?

Who cooked all afternoon?

Who bicycled for wine?

Was your intelligence obvious? Forgiven?

Did you put a hand in the fire?

Did you drive a car into the lake?

Do you want more of a story

as a gift on a postcard to a secret admirer,

as a guard against the fashion, as a volume of trysts,

in a pronouncement of your politics, as a whim,

as a monument to defeat

in a moment when the vanguard upbraids you?

For your time on earth did love

shape you?

Is time passing naturally brutal?

Does it make you think bravely of war,

of the best of civilization in makeshift camps?

Was it a battle of time versus dream,

fought over a dugout of sheets?

Did you account for the dark plastic on the windows?

Did you sleep in your dress?

When did you become old or dead?

Would you behold what is tender and still

when you went in for a kiss

and came out a magnifying glass?

Why go downstairs to read,

weren't you listening to what was said?

Did the end of life make you sad,

so you couldn't write or think?

Isn't it when the strings are taut

you play with complete abandon?

Does no one hear?

OR ELSE?

We sit by a window in April not sure if it's open, if it's spring or summer, and a week or month later, we rub a hole through the glass with the front of our shirt and gin-soaked spit to scrutinize our miserable little body, or else

we dig with teeth and nails through limestone, then nosedive into water until our crown touches ancient Abyssinia. We buy, sell, and trade from the Red Sea to the Nile Valley and amass a fortune in enslaved people and gold, only to die of self-loathing;

or we stand erect at the head of an elaborate cathedral, where we've been named adjudicator of species, dividing those who move to the poles from those who move to the equator, while those drowning in the temperate zones load onto boats with a few eggs and olives;

otherwise we fill our fountain pens with the pulverized vegetables and fruits of our grandparents' meager estates to write of the dysentery and syphilis that marked their passage from east to west, and of our subsequent viral and bacterial passage from west to east, and so on around the globe until the mash runs out and we continue with invisible paper and ink;

or else we pack a slippery ball of wax, and onions and garlic that rot in our wool knapsacks, and board the ear-splitting, speed-of-light jet that ages us but cannot be heard from below and barely appears to move;

up go ballet dancers without tights, marble sculptors missing chisels, first-chair violinists with no bows, maestros with rubber batons, and heartbroken marionettes whose puppeteers are arthritic; with a mighty curiosity, they throw open the portal and commence fly-fishing from clouds, casting nearly weightless lures;

alternatively, we hide in a little waterfall of eminent domain; we whimper, but it is the whimper of princes; we weep, but it is the cry of liberators; we love, but it is a love of words; we rest, but it is the sleep of pagans; we procrastinate, but it is the time of forgiveness; we dig for water, but it is the search for antiquity; we pray, but it is a declaration of independence; we walk, but it is the path to absurdity; we harbor doubts, but they are goats climbing each other's rump; we boat to the middle of the sea, but the sea is in the embrace of the sky.

At seventy, we remember when we were twenty and led horses to far pastures;
now we lead esters of fatty acids and long-chain alcohols into caves of beeswax so the
millennial young may gather inside the honeycomb to discuss philosophy;

we memorize haiku in the early hours, beginning with, "The moon set tonight..." and
continuing, "...over the ruined city; you moved your pillow."

Or else, the bellwether of hell pulls us into the future by a part of nature most untoward,
a chemical trail that cannot, as normal vapor, dissipate; it tows our body as a banner
advertising our grief over our own private beach

that we view with a derangement of senses, morbidly self-centered because our love
has left the world.

At eighty, we embroider our skin with code words and slip through the marketplace—
searching for ourselves when we were thirty—or we open our eyes wide and hide our
tears under our lids; the salt water bathes thousands of memories in a gentle solution.

Otherwise we are hoary, animatronic figures in a nightmare, neither plant nor animal, all
body shell, plastic material, dyed blue hair, and fake purple feathers.

At ninety, our hands shake contrapuntally with traffic passing over a bridge; nothing
moves after a while; then water ruffles under the bridge.

At a hundred, children look like fireflies.

ANIMATRONIC POEM

A few locals loll with their legs stretched. They look dead or relaxed.
The moment before action, were we shooting a scene.

Bowls of guacamole, salsa, and chips hold positions on the low table.
Bouncy Latin music breaks from the player in the armoire.
I surface from my thoughts bloated as a submarine.

A couple spins briefly.
She's wearing an ivory skirt and bright tank top.
Works her hips such that the spaghetti straps droop a little down both arms.
She's having fun. For the first time in a while.
Maybe the world stopped and started again.

Why else is the barbed wire behind the house
notched with pieces of dresses and trousers? A guy with a ponytail, who's been hiding
in the kitchen, occupies the couch with a cola. Rapid-fire laughter.
When asked who you are, say my name. I'd like to do one brave thing
before I'm ashamed.

Somebody shouts. Another holds his finger in one ear and a phone to the other.
His face tight. Are you here hunting for someone?

Squeals accompany the unwrapping of gifts. Paper party dresses hastily removed.
People shoved into the pool.
Spilled salsa, tequila, the past, the future, all hobnobbing.

Do we few who never knew war think of ourselves as political victims?
At any point along a continuum does horror negate life?

FLYING TRAPEZE LESSONS

The moon set tonight
over the ruined city
you moved your pillow

Our leader's pug crapped
on a last bracelet of light
in his crude penthouse

Grinding his stained grin
the short-fingered fascist bids
the moon climb again

Mars fills the lit screen
for our anniversary
in our underpants

Rappers shake floorboards
in a nearby capitol
old male packrats cringe

Doors open doors close
an owl lights on a flagpole
food gone water low

What is a safe night?
Ah!—alert for the quiet
in your giant snore

Hey with our age gap
we make a great cathedral
out of soap bubbles

Burning smells of rain
to fools said the green teacher
who stayed my welcome

Shots fired (in a dream?)
Who goes down, you? A dear friend
loses a shoe running

All about this her
that her in a book I wrote
lightly rustling now

Soft now vigilant
reader hard stares only work
to sneeze at the sun

A tank in the street
sparks a round-up of artists
instead of breakfast

It's never a crime
to miss shadows of late May
fall on a river

Better sixty years
as an oft-confused poet
than one a marksman

PICARESQUE

1

Five people with small axes chop into a cork oak without hurting the tree.

They make a horizontal cut, a crown or necklace on the trunk,

& several vertical fissures to carve out door-sized slabs.

One wipes his young face & glances over at his father,

who pushes the handle of an ax into the opening

so he can peel back the knobby sponge

to the bright, yellow, next living layer of bark,

which will grow back in nine years,

when his father will allow him the delicate maneuver.

Now the boy stacks the planks in the forest.

I'm thinking as I drive to the movies

that our carpet needs to be replaced,

rethought altogether, & what with screw caps

better to stopper wine, the under-harvested cork

is environmentally correct enough,

imported from the Old World through Miami—

it's another dark summer day in an American head.

2

I park for the cheap Tuesday show. It's 102 degrees, climbing to 106.

I ascend a suburban mountain of steps, a copy of the great pyramid at Chichén Itzá, postmenopausally-challenging rungs laid stone by stone by Mayan astrophysicists,

from whom many of my neighbors descend, a thousand years before "we" discovered the New World.

I finally reach the mythical city of the lobby, exhausted.

It is rich in stained, springless couches, fluorescent light, & imitation adobe brick, painfully white, spidery & greasy.

Arriving early, I check my email & phone messages, none, none.

Now showing: Victorian period piece starring Carey Mulligan, *Far from the Madding Crowd.*

Poor Thomas Hardy,

in charge of the excavation of a graveyard as a young man. Never at home in London in his beautiful ruby of a brain.

He pines for his first wife, dead Emma, even after marriage to his secretary, thirty-nine years younger. He's devoted to poetry,

even after success with characters struggling against social circumstances & passions,

as my darling also struggles at home with creation, drawing uncircumcised penises & uteruses for her show *Both And.*

I must remember to call Pest Control because of roaches partying in the pantry.

We've got a hinge broken on the oven & a retired, small snake in our pool. The pool is an advantage of the middle class in this misbegotten desert,

& the required fence around the pool a reminder of the fence along the border with Mexico that I've built, against my will, with tax dollars. I struggle vainly with my developing character,

3

even though she is only at the movies

& not alone with her thoughts

nor with her hands on a small ax in a forest,

nor with her torso on a section of barbed fence.

She is a permanently older, temporarily safe American,

not particularly noticed as a tank-topped lesbian

nor discriminated against today. She is rarely seen at all,

whereas her assets are on display, not, as once was thought,

on her body, but as the pool in the yard, stressing the current,

& worsening, water shortage & coeval guilt.

 "Assets" are a "product" her family "explored,"

the way conquerors gnawed through the Americas.

Their descendant, clearly one-eighth the size of creatures

on a silver screen, settles next to a blinding vending machine.

She is not here to chew or be chewed out, professionally

or otherwise. She might as well be in a boiler room selling penny stocks

& placing private, illegal orders alongside her brother.

Indolently, privileged-ly at the theater, best to hold the door open

for a misplaced actor, or hack into it delicately with an ax

& peel back a bright, sweaty, living meaning.

4

A group of seven or eight rolls in, led by a dedicated health services worker, nearly
undressed (because summer),

but they don't notice me. It feels hellish feeling sorry,

in a world where mobilization counts for so much, that these souls are being wheeled &
whirled about. It's pitiful doling out pity, especially when intended

for a clock ticking in an optimist's shop shuttered at the far end of this mall. It's a short
hop, which maneuver one takes terribly for granted,

to self-pity, because one planned to be a hula hoop champion or tree climber,
but now exercises stock options, giving the buyer rights but not obligations.

The lobby's air-conditioning slaves away, low on the ethereal gas for which no substitute
refrigerant exists. Our father, indentured to us, owned a coolant business in the Bronx;
he'd come home smelling faintly sweet of toxin.

The boy in the story has to borrow his father's handkerchief in the high heat and low
humidity necessary to grow the cork, and the cheap dye comes off blue on his face.

While I perspire in a quiet corner of the vestibule,

waiting for the film to end so as to start it from the beginning in case it is Hardy's
masterpiece,

the shaggy Almighty Himself hypes *DIOS ES BUENO* from a blue-eyed poster,

and to Our Lord's left, an ancient speaker of computerized jackhammers

heralds, at this appointed hour, a new catastrophe release. Going deaf, with no
disrespect,

I trade the waiting for the screening room, where, with what one

can only assume is spiritual intervention, a synthesizer unlooses a terrorizing pitch.

A patron undone by the war zone in the lobby, relocated & so inclined against the now
shredding & screaming bionic violin

may hold his or her ears for dear life,

simply the two of us as if we are dating, me & a dedicated, theoretically naked social worker, with index fingers deep into the vents of our ears

& his eyes squinched like two miniature accordions out of breath. Looks like a very nice guy.

5

Curtain closes. Previews still running, the unworthy assault cuts off.

Unwashed patrons in wheelchairs are verbalizing various celestial sounds.

Curtain rises. Commercial rolling, music storms back in. On, off, up, down.

How often does this happen?

Six, possibly seven times.

I check my phone messages again:

something about a friend driving her 95-year-old father to somebody's funeral.

Something's not right with that.

& by that I mean: curtain rises, curtain falls again.

Having arrived an hour early on purpose, to get out of the house so as to appear

to have somewhere to go,

this is what I'm writing because I don't write anymore:

the carpet is aging—Portuguese cork, cost?—& roaches keep vandalizing the pantry.

6

Poor Hardy, couldn't get his first poetry collection published until age fifty-eight.

His heart is buried with Emma, his ashes in Poets' Corner. Couldn't be one with the universe, even in death.

Although I haven't crossed parts of Mexico without hydrating, as some in this establishment who clean up illegally after the show, I'm terribly thirsty without my fizz pop.

Curtain up.
At last, the infertile British moor.

Carey Mulligan, how lovely, flinty, & young you are.

The plot thickens with multiple rejected marriage proposals & reversals of fortune;

at some point, a wife pries open the coffin of her husband's first love,

but the sad, genuine moment belongs to the fortyish bachelor courting Bathsheba,
whose false valentine awakens & destroys him. Murder, mayhem—the usual,
albeit great, novel.

Why, I think, is it not *maddening*, but rather, *madding*? I will look it up now that the
house lights are lit.

I'd prefer to go home, but have I lain low long enough for my young lover to enjoy her
own company?

Carey Mulligan, do you watch your early movies, even though you are only thirty, only
recently an errand-runner & barmaid?

Searching for a dictionary, I open a window of my cell, a prisoner with superpower.

I find instead a self-portrait squinting into sunlight, with the reprimand of my mother on
its face, feeling about me as I feel about the effluvia in this underground garage & the
manure on that moor. But there is love,

as the sweaty, state-sanctioned caregiver/driver straps each individual into his, her, &
their seatbelt,

as delicately and distractedly as a chef laying in shopping bags from the greengrocer,

& each individual's wheelchair into the rump of a van. *There was an old woman who
lived in a shoe* crackles in surround sound in my mind while I shrink

7

into the rear of my vehicle, reviewing, as I would a performance,

my life, pausing right before rain in an early spring

twenty or thirty years ago. I feel invisible,

or indivisible, I can't decide which, I guess I'll look that up, too.

The humidity is profound in memory. Clouds above April

barely bodied, smeared with kohl, float as in a fashion show

in slow motion, exquisitely cared-for racehorses

out of mythology. They're merely gods, in shapely ideas

about desire, dressed as women whom I would love

to binge-watch, clearly a drama

some aging babycakes such as myself should skip.

For the finale,

8

I am captured in a Peruvian villager's cone-shaped hat, whose earflaps tie under my chin with colored, braided strings, so I can't hear anymore, but I truly care to.

I remember native peoples of the high Andes wearing such hats in a painting, infantilized & immortalized in a colorful pastoral with a parade in the foreground,

goats & cows higher up, flute players & a drum master off to the right in Brueghel-busy oblivion, while, at the top, smaller but most important, Atahualpa, the last sovereign emperor before the Spanish conquest, who,

upon being taken hostage, offers the Spaniards enough gold to fill the room he is imprisoned in. A marketplace crackles

with clowns on horseback & kids on goats' teats, also spices, potatoes, & docile guinea pigs for sale, which, squashed under stones & fried for dinner, are prized rodents, which, from higher on the list of privileged species, a lesbian looks down upon.

Plus, in the artist's rendering, portly caricatures finally enjoy a day off from actual
shoeing & milking. They bustle along the parade route in bright wool attire

& in the conical chullo of my inanity & their ancestors, with more than a few copying
the bowler hats of British railway workers, introduced into the country in 1920,

when these unarmed invaders apprehended the interior. Our painter, Gabriel Cuyo,
with more divine intervention, evidently also took liberties with history,

9

as a daydreamer is wont to do

in the market of the Sacred Valley

under the tawny skirts of the foothills

buying pink salt & chocolate &

pigments for my darling. I'm patronizing

because it seems only today

I scaled above the lost tourists of Machu Picchu

to look down upon—literally—a great,

ruined civilization. If the villagers were alive,

it would be a privilege to be alive.

Perhaps I believe instinctively that I'm not

doing some good, not living

a life of right conduct. Like, I could

be writing an animated film

starring a pineapple of extra energy

& donating the billions to charity.

Against advice by the wise

to Let Three Days Pass

before tendering a plan,

I let three cars pass

before pushing through an exit

on the freeway in a loathsome state

of silent alarm, home.

WHITE POPPIES AND PURPLE THISTLES

Somebody's son is lifted
from the ground onto a burned table
in a terribly blue body.
Along with the prettiest purple and blue vetch.
Without his priest or shot of whiskey.
Wags an overgrown beard worse off
than a bunch of diseased grapes.

True enough going to die

Another miserable day in the field
for Pedanius Dioscorides
with the Roman army.
What with needing to hack
the heavy boy's bad leg
with no painkillers.

And I kept warning you and you believed me

The earth heats up.
The Greek pharmacologist and botanist saws.
Senses the good soldier will go very hot
and metal cold. Surrounded by white
papery prickly poppies with bright yellow eyes.
Which will be a cure for cloudy sight.
But aren't going to help this poor kid.
He isn't to see anything for very long.
Who presently is bawling his eyes out
when he isn't screeching and begging

What are you doing

here with me recounting a distant morning
of low clouds and crosswinds. A few stray sounds.
Teen legionaries softened out of respect
for the dying. You quiet too for a moment
of ancient characters under an ill-fitting
metallic sky. Slowly lifts like a helmet
off a dead boy with a sunny smile.

When you get out of bed it's already afternoon   The sleep of the young

The boy is not Achilles in the *Iliad*
who Dioscorides knows
can stop himself bleeding in the wild

with feathered yarrow flowers.
Today's leg has been tossed
next to a pissing horse.

Life is three weeks of rare butterflies and then nothing

The doctor slumps onto a pile
of mud-colored dried hide.
A mother has to live through
news that her boy's leg snaps off
like a stout thistle underfoot.
And that's if the exhausted messenger
on a dehydrated horse can find her.
Already weeping under some smelly hay.

Time passes over tragedies equally

While an emperor recites poems with a lyre
many handsome enemies badmouthing him
die burnt as invasive sumac at the banquet.
Paroled in time for the pelagic void.
Wherein Nero gifts his mother a yacht

Lit by flares

rigged to collapse on her.
Hears of her swimming ashore
only to order Agrippina greeted
with a stab to the womb.
It turns pearlescent in the morning

A cheerful feeling not recognizing what's coming

in the very month before the eternal
city burns to matchsticks and twigs.
If a Jew isn't caught burying the torch
lay it in a Christian's hand.
Bloody war and palace intrigue.

We escape through ranch country

Up a narrow airless path
onto a ridge with this century's friends.
Yarrow and poppy along
a Sonoita winery. Sad
oxymoron between desert
mountains closing in. Nobody cares

Terrified to be dead without you

whether a few diehard poets
tasting and ballyhooing in baggy pants
with red splashes on our chests

get gone for a day from war
and humiliation in America. We fail
to help somebody shot in a far city.
Another overdosing on meth.

Shame on us in the middle

Of nowhere. She's face up in vetch.
He's face down on a futon.
Who's squeezing their loosening grips?
Pastureland as far as the eye can wander
out of a cataract. I really don't want to die
today. As simply a poppy in an open trench.
But if I have to, it would be fair that I am
so much older than you.

One should die in a protected order

The notables in this poem are patient enough
not to leave you asleep as one of the grasses
in a hay bed. Likely as not lonely
you'll meet somebody else. Never forget
I want you to. It's better, in a desert radiant
of nuclear immanence, to beg
a love without hurt
from an inspired humble society.

Than be bitter

I've lived into my sixties
and failed my countrymen.
Burning lights at night
as captives dipped in oil
set ablaze to illumine
Nero's garden.
Whether it's true or not
is beside the point.
As one forgives
one bleeds out.

Not going to make it

39

SHELTER IN PLACE

Should I presume a bleak day signaling rain, or rather a fine finale that I broker for
another morning, another slow-poured afternoon, and one night, streaked by peach tree
branches, one more full moon from my window?
Do you break from painting into the damaged world of the living room,
from my crooked look conclude that my face resembles my missing parents', clots of each
dotting the white sky of a distant city?
Is it another night, by happenstance my last?
O am I seized? O shit,
does the philanthropic instant grant that I lurch and land on you?
Is it the bit when a leg of a chair under you gives way, pretty comic, except if you're
pregnant or dying?
Did the two left feet of my moonwalk bruise your fleshy and wondrous figure?
And how unprepared your wide eyes are for my gaze so steady and so far.

By hazy dawn you sleep apart.
I keep getting farther away, even though I'd rather stretch my bones and blow words
through my mouth again. Death fuses a handlebar
too loosely to its frame, poorly casts a shank of engine metal, cancers a mole, leaks toxin
into a vent, and sets down a tornado into a point of green earth, until it's no longer
necessary to avoid mirrors to avoid aging.
Was it a matter of civility that I deserved any time at all with you? an accident?
I stepped across a spiny bridge and iron desert, and before I knew it, an unfamiliar
landscape rose, flowering in violet light. I hate it.
Did you find your shoes after a terrible mist and climb straight up your goat mountain?

WHETHER THE GOAT IS A METAPHOR

We go on talking and digging a pit in the earth
to spit-roast kid,
since anyone working in a lively rhythm is not attached
to the story.
In saving her, he saves himself.
It's getting late.
The story of the boy is that
by drinking water from a hoof, he's turned into a goat.
If we separate magic from life,
we get art. His sister, long story short,
gets thrown into a river with a stone around her neck.
His weeping stirs the neighbors with a silken net
to scoop her out. He turns three somersaults
of joy and lands on two feet as a boy again.
How, in heaven's name, will dinner be served, and when?
Separate art from life, we get nothing.
We go on talking and digging.
I've got a million and ten things to do.
Of the multitude of things, it is emptiness
that's necessary now, now that you've had time
to wash and dress. As a form
of enlightenment, the most unsuspecting guest
is your enemy in armor, or invisible,
who will clap you on the back
when you choke on a bone at the banquet.

NAMASTE, Y'ALL

Terrible Buddhists! How I miss you!

If a child you don't know won't say hello to you

what does that say?

If you are pecked by a crow on the way home

for no good reason circling the river walk

what do you and the crow know?

If you inquire about the state of the art

but the artist is the worst character in the city

where is the first bus to the coast?

Hearing a king fart in his pissant mansion

why be surprised strolling by that

his wax effigy melts in the park?

If you are charged for parts and labor

but own no car

why argue the bill of fare?

If you have a conversation with your mother

in your head because she's dead

why have you lost your sense of humor?

If you are at the governor's ball

completely undressed, why not

drink the bubbly?

If you stand under a small live oak

confused for an olive, are you

or the oak confused for an olive?

(When is an olive not confused for a live oak?

When you have it in your mouth, silly!)

Why are you at a night at the opera,

if you hate opera and the civilization

that spawned it, rather than at a brawl?

If you are dragooned into living with a despot

with a full belly, is yours or his full, or both,

and if you refuse but garlic and onion,

how will you spy for the opposition?

When you hear the phrase *hog heaven,*

but are a vegetarian, are you smug and pink?

blue and unfulfilled? dark and indulgent?

For a Jew in this culture, are you pleasantly surprised

to see family under the mistletoe in June?

Why do both cousins praise jasmine

when you invite them for dinner in winter

with tempests in trench coats and hoods

howling from the east, filling a city block

with their black stretch limousine?

If you are enamored of the weirdest gadgets,

but have forsworn the media and the church, why are you

tempted by candles and chants? Why ask

where the full moon has gone if you've switched windows?

Terrible Buddhists! How I love you!

LASER

We don't choose hope. We choose words.

That would be us. A darkness of midday

for the helpless and dispossessed.

Our earthlessness is years

not eons away. Of the first people,

someone careens up the steep driveway, drops off

a package, and leaves

to write *of* outdoors, under the assumption

that nature prevails.

Is that the phrase

to spread an old Russian shawl to write outdoors?

As skywriting, some words briefly quiver

after great noise and speed.

It could be said we hallucinate

friezes onto a refrigerator-white wall

for environmental advantage.

A creamy young light goes off

with the pagan gods of daily life

to fret about history and virtue. As a dog

the empty space

absorbs a gold couch

as proof

of a long-lost story

we stare stupidly

into the world's furnace

until we see ourselves

as charcoal in it

I may open the door

in a day or two

it's summer

a delicious wind

of the last few

air-conditioned

until the darkness shreds

its veil tomorrow

renewing an intimacy

I bury myself

scratches a dirt floor,

we scrape womb-shaped lamps

to plant new bulbs.

No one reads anymore.

Hat pulled tight,

no one drives over

stiff hoses in the burnt yard.

That's when

sunlight traverses unequivocally

between a soul and a body.

in an old notebook

of thirty years ago

mostly quotes from others

poetry it's just

you can thank God

a few loose pages

only to find

they're not body parts not yet

we'll know

the difference

not much

WHAT IS VIRTUE?

The police received a report of a disturbance

A stab of daylight
Punctures the crime scene
Seeking the virtuous life you imagine

Maybe they ate together
Maybe they hadn't seen each other for a while
The leavings

Of wisdom and serenity
Tortilla scraps and cabbage strips
Lay cool and hard after lunch

A suspect has been described by a witness
Has he been found
Out in the world lost to you?

Approximately age 30
With dreadlocks and a do-rag
A man forced to be compliant to law

Can he grasp the law as easily
As a knife in a kitchen drawer?
Righteously aggrieved words fail

A woman beyond her limits
May 23rd high of 85 degrees
Torn as slashes in a tablecloth

She may have leaned over awhile
In a sheer fabric of shock
Between good and evil

Two thousand years of trading in the laws
Of temperance and self-sacrifice
Forsake his rage her fear his fear her rage his

Boiled over like a soup pot of stew meat
This is provided as a timely warning
Whatever was deferred in his body

A blue muscle shirt with campus logo
Towered over its object and bled out
Onto a sunny sleeveless shift

Bad weather on the way
She had just washed and ironed
Danced a little in her own skin

To Beyoncé's prophecy "Pretty Hurts"
The hour was intended to be spent
Freely as an afternoon at the movies

Soon it will be mopped down with vinegar
Aggravated assault 2000 block of Whitis Avenue
Two big soft drinks for air-conditioning

Nearby Eastwoods Park and Wading Pool
Police cars at the location
Drive around ten quail babies you bet eight or nine will be eaten

This situation is being fleshed out
An angry male six feet tall and two hundred ninety pounds
Swiped clean of hot sauce with a flowery napkin

Armed with a knife stood up and opened her chest No
One overreaction accounts for the wounds
As reported by a neighbor

First there seemed a cheerful feeling in the street
Second report at the location 1:03 p.m.
Then the bone-chilling

Nearly to zero to bare my responsibility
My present habit of composing has to do
With the flaws in the paper

The suspect fled on foot
After cutting her up pretty badly
Should you be reading the account

Phone 911
When you learn the subject is white and you
If you're white figured otherwise

You have to own that
Your racial bias is fucked as a jaw out of whack
For so long you think it feels right

This not being
Unusual in a primitive society
Suspect and victim are known

What is not apprehended at this time is
That power is somebody's son
"God's son" somebody said neighbors gather

For spiritual purposes
A black male stands back from the scene of the crime
If you are black perhaps you feel relief

If you see the suspect
Anyone dark emerges looking over his shoulder
Paranoid in a white neighborhood

Nothing personal whispered
After a long weekend of rising humidity
His behavior is assumed suspicious

Everybody's underwear sticking to him
As insects to flypaper
In historically Southern rooms

The past is a torn sheet
Of racial profiling
And gender defiling

Should you be listening to the chatter
Do not attempt to approach extreme danger
Is violence when people cannot assume

Their attendant talents in a storied civil society?
Do not stand down
This is a developing situation

Let's cut to the chase
People with information immediately alert police
Running into an alley weapons drawn

What are they capable of triggering?
Names shall be redacted before trial
In any case

No one wants to assume *the woman's identity*
We learn that *she works downtown*
Also she's close to her grandmother

Who can't find a ride to the hospital
A cat or a dog reported squealing
A virtuous society would allow for a fair fight

But when the curtain is drawn back on the empire
We have lost consciousness
Of pure form

Thunderstorms expected in the afternoon

THE VOWEL WITH SHORTNESS OF BREATH HIKES UP THE DEEPLY GUARDED SECRET

Spring in February blossoms with the lilacs of a simpler time—smell them?
Similar to cherry soda and hard purple suckers, those dissolving sugars?
Are you straggling home from softball chewing the same stick of gum?
Did you leave your metal lunch box at school?
Child, freckled lifting off your T-shirt in the humidity?
Throw a pink ball into the sky and where will it land? Here,
with a green mitt in your hand? Tomboy,
is it a rare day unattended by parents who have gone to the city?

Can you believe no one ignores you at the dance after all?
Isn't this where you kissed your first girl, or where you wanted to?
By the willow behind the suburbs? Was someone raped there later?
Can the warm weather open the victim's claim like a window? Why can't we
help her? A red biplane coasts overhead on a Sunday afternoon, see it?
The shiver of traffic resumes after an ambulance passes—did you hold your ears?

WHETHER THE FAMILY DESERVES SYMPATHY

The family deploys ketchup on soft spaghetti or laminates other meals
The young girl pokes around a few radishes and a chopped head of lettuce
Bullying a tomato unripe as a padded vinyl seat
Bruised up against a Formica table from this Her Majesty's throne
A late afternoon winter sun spills over the horizon of her plate

Out the picture window neighbors smoking huddle faithfully
They ape a winning football team about to throw the game
A Mafia failure with a big Oldsmobile barks at them
His wife skinny as a lost dog out on the street of an evening
Nobody so much as opens a shade to admit her life is in serious danger

Over the gossip about *the dago and his bitch*
A mother points with a kitchen knife to lord over the ferocious little animal
Who's being told eat dammit before you explain your poor behavior
Do not get up from this table without a clean plate don't you understand how hard I work
Why can't you listen to me like your brother he doesn't back-talk

Her holler goes one-way on its abacus over a skull of frostbitten ice cream
Beyond the hybrid willows of twilight her charge escapes quietly
As a star rising over a raging fire
Our pillow of tears is a cloudburst from the cosmos
By day a landfill of choplogic rises between beds

Where the siblings play with rolled-up socks and scorecards
They hang a necklace of wire on their closet door for his free throws
From the foul line she has to retrieve the mock ball *woof woof* good girl
Up ahead where even a dog won't go because of the electric fence
The brother says I need to siphon a shit-ton of money

Off from this family that you'll never see again
In the classic storybook
They mop their prince's stallion with ammonia
This old drama's ending will be tragicomic
As the parents are perennially enchanted

By their son's ginned-up story about making good
The carcass of his many postdated checks
Lay uncashed in mother's peeling nightstand
When she died over it
She had displayed diamond-encrusted costume jewelry

She always said you've got to prepare for a rainy day
She sure in hell knew wasn't real
Before she was lights out
She reminded me to recover cash stashed between folded towels
Another Plan B fandango of hers but afterward I had to hire a stranger

To go through her pretty underthings I couldn't handle them or the rack
Of suits and nighties disembodied neat as meat hanging in a locker
I found a bare bones note Janie what's left is yours
I'm not going to lie
Unearthing her spindly handwriting a cleaver of cheerful feeling came over me

Outside I fell to pieces in dead leaves as stiff as her expired potato chips
Inside again I tore open that old bag and drained a beer
As cold and refreshing as a waterfall
Walking around naked it fell to me
To forgive mother's sword and brother's orders

As they forgive these fighting words not any more or less serious
Than any other practice made of metal, cloth, fiber, rubber, wood, and paper
That is a good reminder childhood is a construct
A puppet show in a toy theater
And you try not to be moved to tears by the part love plays

QUIET MIND

Was it a psychotic break

    when our sweetheart cried out

        I'm giving birth I'm breaching

in that barren farmhouse

    of borrowed furniture

        and bruising electric guitars

and she wasn't desperate

    but you could tell it wasn't good

        icicles breaking off our roof

shot spears through fresh snow

    we'd been carrying on

        on and off all year

the two of us rarely alone

    more or less beleaguered

        and excited both

still young and confused

    sensitive but limited

        as a pet or friend

that couldn't help

    but be scared

        of the aftermath

a broken leg a broken heart

    stoned flirting with politics

        at parties crammed into

tight leather pants

    we blew through the cocked night

        riding sex toys into the sunrise

what part of culture

did we ignore

      a triumvirate of crippled horses

the psychosexual

     the legal the perverse

      to share a lover unplugged

on drugs strapped to her

     guitar she sang a secret language

      she wore a Chinese dragon

embroidered on her jacket

     maybe it was all the rage

      it was ok we said love

snow piled immediately

     after it was plowed

      out of our element

we said experiment

     out of our minds

      into hers briefly

I am so sorry so so

     sad because I'll never learn

      whether it was her toasted

self out of control or my god

     her few friends that we did did we not

      recognize what was at stake

the all but involuntary

     soul escaping the rented house

      a developing consciousness

of having mistaken pain

     for beauty I would have given you

      completely to her if I thought

that would help if I had

     the power but what was it

she wanted neither

of us stayed around

to inquire after the affair

her parents collected her

a newborn in a cast

lifting her into their car

I drove a thousand miles

in reverse while the wind spun

me vainly toward enlightenment

a tornado funneled into the heartland

but you had a way of forgiving too fine a point

years later when I saw her

at a friend's funeral rehashing

the old garbled days laughing

that high laugh that was sexy

and crazy throwing her bright hair

around and lowering her smoky eyes

to her body I had assumed

dead in jail or brain-dead

in a mental ward maybe

selling drugs maybe married

definitely not ours I hardly owned

what I used to call brainlessly

her white-girl looks gone whatever

I'd thought strawberry blond signaled

a misprision worsened by my driving her home

long ago to our overheated bed

becoming the chattel of memory

we burned leftovers and cigarettes

inside of an hour

the cabin was an oven

so naturally

      I attended to her mille feuille

           after fanfaronading about ethics

for about sixty seconds

      we had only just spoken briefly

           while you curled as a nautilus in your country

it was as if words weren't to be

      wasted on her it was as if I were

           some sicko I didn't really want to save

her beside ourselves orgasmic and weepy

      I lost count I nearly passed out from her

           slow circling

o merry go-round

      whose axis quivered mercifully awhile

           there upon my weary mount

I was taken for a ride

      longer than I'd meant

           which totally deconstructed

a few obligatory ideas I'd held

      regarding scarcity and fecundity

           aka heaven and hell

hot as a stupid stripper pole

      I plummeted immoderately

           from a pouty mouth

to unlit fluted lips

      curled fondant another weakness for dessert

           late in the afternoon

I ought not to have hurried

      her out I'm embarrassed and ashamed

           by the response feigned

indifference I can't imagine

      what the attraction was about

or more exactly what part of myself

called forth needed to be made whole

by going on to share her with you I didn't need to

understand I simply needed not to die

in a ringing cold place once I knew

she was alive and well I heard her saying

how she had enjoyed our company

enough at the funeral it hit me

with a smack to my head that I could give her

up forever but I would never

allow how it was that I lost you the one

susurration that quiets my mind love

isn't any longer a question

of fire but the cure for it

salved onto the liver-spotted

days and nights of my sixties

madness Winnicott wrote is a need

to be believed the disturbance in the air

a hawk flapping its wings furiously

endured for years after I thought of us

as a crashed fuselage in the fallows

why was it

countermanding bossy fate

I was crazy restless

for the cold to come on

did our mothers not care

for us did our fathers not prepare us

or was it the kind of passion that was just

as you said temporary insanity

hush now that question exists

in the larger social context of mind

SPACE, LIGHT, AND A BLUE CYCLORAMA

The cosmos answers an owl in a fig tree!
Once I was loved by a woman who,
while canoodling amiss, acted as if I had
the only heart who mattered. And I believed it.
But I sat around crying anyway. I would receive love
letters from her as if nothing had happened.
Maybe nothing had. The life you might have lived,
which you still remember, is composed of the soft,
metaphysical murmurs of the world.
You wander through the desert on a quest
for a ring of white petals on the head of a stranger.
There it is, a saguaro in bloom.
The difference between poetry and prose is that
today is clanging along very slowly very fast,
while the official tableau is outside of time, hushed.

·

Love is asleep. My darling dreams that
I lose my mind in a restaurant's powder room.
When we leave after the meal, it's still light.
I take the wheel because she's on the phone.
She's on the phone when she realizes
I'm driving off the road. Then perpendicularly,
to correct the mistake. I manage a U-turn
and set the car by the opposite side.
By now, she's red-faced. Also, I exited
the restroom with my hair soaking wet,
but she hasn't had a chance to ask about that.
Tenderness has a million questions it can't answer.

THE DOODLIN' WALLIHOPS

Are you pouring drinks for an acquaintance? Driving faster without me in the car?

Are we sleeping on board when I let go your hand?

From a towel on the sand am I watching you surf, or planning a trip without

luggage or you? Living in capitals not calling you?

Is that you at a border and me with a cardboard sign on the other side? Or am I rich,

retired, reading, and not once thinking of you?

Hey, even if I'm stranded with the last cow in a barn,

or writing poetry that is so lonely, and fighting with you in my idiot head,

you are my heartland, Texan, partner, slow-smoked ribs,

habanero pepper, chicken fried steak, my great doodlin' wallihop, my dinner date—

Did you say you'd be late?

Are you locking up soundlessly, then burying all morning in a feather quilt,

wearing headphones with new music? Laughing so hard with your sister?

Have you left me hanging the hundred chandeliers

of romance, missing a deadline without your assist, losing sleep because of your snore,

making love, eyes shuttered, coming apart?

Quickly, which is more effortless, *before* swimming the river with you among maidenhair

ferns, or *after,* stepping off cliff's edge and slipping your grasp?

Did you see, or miss, that sweet donkey?

I drive our street in shade between buildings awash in the moon.

Isn't that where, alone in the afternoon, lovers go?

You'll be an old woman I'll never know. My doodlin' wallihop,

after I die, are you at home painting the sky?

FAITH

Dare I expect nothing more after You seized my suckered father and stressed mother

and nearly broke Fred's back over a few bankruptcies?

In response am I made to play the most ignominious part in the pantomime, the horse's

ass?

Or is there a terrible misunderstanding about what is, in fact, a whore's bath in a motel?

Why wash me with a damp cloth?

Does seeing me involve wanting your money back from a freak show starring yours truly,

with the camera zeroed in on your poor subject's mistake, to have craved the right

person for the wrong reason? Did I betray You

by drifting in the bug spray of the past or far ahead without figuring how to get through

the shitty day? It happens a billion times,

but no one attends the funeral with as many guard dogs as You. Why make me feel scared

among familiars? Should we assume your biggest mistake, lying awake in a shroud

until somebody cherishes us

again? But for an hour is that You

leaving children at home, aware the designated isn't quite old enough to be in charge?

Are You driving across town to do the majestic thing of not looking

away from the implosion?

It seems to breathe a little life into us dummies with the certainty of a torpedo, no? *No,*

You say, *it's nothing for them to be alone, the children will be ok,*

it's you I'm worried about.

So that would be You examining me with the hard stare of the connoisseur who

understands the material to be inferior?

Do You wipe our faces with your face because You are a great friend of vainglory?

If we live in ignorance as a Martian on a half shell, do we get to die in peace, or else,

against your will, shall we set all our desire?

How would it be to sleep and wake in that place whose transient neon flickers, *If you*

want to feel better, don't let your suffering protect you?

THE DISCLOSURE OF THE MOON BY ITS SENTRIES

1

Those of you on the earth, a blue and green wash of your collective breaths,

why is it that you appeal to something or someone above you, are we not your equal
and your companion? Often we ask ourselves,

why do we bear your curiosities, your poetry launched toward the heavens as so many
manned and empty ships moored, unmoored, and abandoned? Are they not trophies that
are better buried, or, better yet, unsent?

How are we to bear your fear, which rockets toward us even as it backfires?

We are not your gods, nor your watchdogs, can't you tell that we are simply dreaming
as you dream, awakened every time you land on us with a violence that reverberates
forever as poor rocks, upset dusts without seas and grasses?

How do you feel when you don't bathe in our light for a few hours of an evening on Earth
with your arm around your date?

Is the full moon on clear mornings a lost ring filled with your expectations? While you
appear not to understand

our gaze upon you, which is merely a brush with experience, how do you think it feels
to be exposed by mighty telescopes, as if you're a pervert at a keyhole?

By a lake of lazy, multiplying algae, or an ocean edged with a hard, deteriorating ribbon
of coral, you gaze with a longing out of all proportion to our light, indifferent touch. Is it
moonlessness

in particular that you ambush because from emptiness you seem to squeeze
the greatest meaning?

Stranger, we only ask, because we're loyal and hospitable, what do you crave first
when you arrive—is it taste? So, will you taste your honeydew now?

2

Does spring or summer feel early?

Is that why you pool your feelings in ice, and why you store your ideas in a sieve?

Has a memory returned to you, is that from childhood, or invented?
We miss the beehives of love, too few to perish.
(Was that *too few* or *too true*?)

You act so out of sorts,
is your restlessness your trust issue? For our part, we would rather not have to move again.

Will you apply your considerable experience of language and things to us?

(Please don't make too much of our darkness)

Do the purples and creams of nature console, or do thoughts of hyacinths and bluebells confuse you? Do lilacs prove you had a soul?

(Cross the great basalt slowly) (There is no trading for other questions)

Do you grasp how the list got cut off after worm, rose, turtle, and leaf?

And that we have nothing to do with it, without a care in the world?

Can you accept that without time
you are really the only pilgrim here, space trash forever?

Where does that leave you? Dressed, undressed, ready or not,
do you regard your recent shift as a newly discovered idea?

Did you notice any monsters? (No need to answer)
With knives in their throats?

Is your guilt or innocence a concern?
(This is not a trade for sex or request for confession)
(No blade is involved at all)

Are you making your own inquiry? Because absent a body

you have to ask yourself, who's there?

If the last thing there is the first here, will spirit be enough?

Do you know the future without you
doesn't hurt? (The knife is rubber)

Are you prepared to guard nothing rather than something?

ABOUT THE AUTHOR

Jane Miller is the author of twelve books of poetry and a collection of essays on poetry, culture, and travel. She taught graduate and undergraduate poetry workshops and seminars for many years as a professor at the University of Arizona, serving for a time as MFA program director, and is currently a visiting writer with the Michener Center at the University of Texas, Austin. She lives in Tucson with the artist Valyntina Grenier.